Memories

John Galsworthy, Maud Earl

MEMORIES

MEMORIES

BY

JOHN GALSWORTHY

ILLUSTRATED BY
MAUD EARL

NEW YORK
CHARLES SCRIBNER'S SONS
1914

First published in ' The Inn of Tranquillity, October, 1912
New Impressions December, 1912, February, March, 1913,
February, 1914
Separate Illustrated Edition November, 1914

TO
JOHN WALLER HILLS

ILLUSTRATIONS

ILLUSTRATIONS

MEMORIES

MEMORIES

WE set out to meet him at Waterloo Station on a dull day of February— I, who had owned his impetuous mother, knowing a little what to expect, while to my companion he would be all original. We stood there waiting (for the Salisbury train was late), and wondering with a warm, half-fearful eagerness what sort of new thread Life was going to twine into our skein. I think our chief dread was that he might have light eyes—those yellow Chinese eyes of the common, parti-coloured spaniel And each new minute of the train's tardiness increased our anxious compassion: his first journey; his first separation from his mother; this black two-months' baby! Then the train ran in, and we hastened to look for him. " Have you a dog for us ? "

" A dog! Not in this van. Ask the rear-guard."

" Have you a dog for us ? "

" That's right. From Salisbury. Here's your wild beast, sir ! "

From behind a wooden crate we saw a long black-muzzled nose poking round at us, and heard a faint hoarse whimpering.

I remember my first thought:

" Isn't his nose too long ? "

But to my companion's heart it went at once, because it was swollen from crying and being pressed against things that he could not see through. We took him out—soft, wobbly, tearful, set him down on his four, as yet not

"Here's your wild beast, Sir!"

"We took him out — soft, wobbly, tearful;"

quite simultaneous legs, and regarded him.
Or, rather, my companion did, having her head
on one side, and a quavering smile; and I
regarded her, knowing that I should thereby
get a truer impression of him.

He wandered a little round our legs, neither
wagging his tail nor licking at our hands; then
he looked up, and my companion said · " He's
an angel!"

I was not so certain.   He seemed hammer-
headed, with no eyes at all, and little connection
between his head, his body, and his legs.   His
ears were very long, as long as his poor nose;
and gleaming down in the blackness of him I
could see the same white star that disgraced his
mother's chest

Picking him up, we carried him to a four-
wheeled cab, and took his muzzle off.   His

little dark-brown eyes were resolutely fixed on distance, and by his refusal to even smell the biscuits we had brought to make him happy, we knew that the human being had not yet come into a life that had contained so far only a mother, a wood-shed, and four other soft, wobbly, black, hammer-headed angels, smelling of themselves, and warmth, and wood shavings. It was pleasant to feel that to us he would surrender an untouched love, that is, if he would surrender anything. Suppose he did not take to us !

And just then something must have stirred in him, for he turned up his swollen nose and stared at my companion, and a little later rubbed the dry pinkness of his tongue against my thumb. In that look, and that unconscious restless lick, he was trying hard to leave un-

"Four other soft, wobbly, black, hammer-headed angels,"

MEMORIES

happiness behind, trying hard to feel that these
new creatures with stroking paws and queer
scents, were his mother, yet all the time he
knew, I am sure, that they were something
bigger, more permanently, desperately his.
The first sense of being owned, perhaps (who
knows) of owning, had stirred in him. He
would never again be quite the same unconscious creature.

A little way from the end of our journey we
got out and dismissed the cab. He could
not too soon know the scents and pavements of
this London where the chief of his life must
pass. I can see now his first bumble down
that wide, back-water of a street, how continually and suddenly he sat down to make sure
of his own legs, how continually he lost our
heels. He showed us then in full perfection

what was afterwards to be an inconvenient—
if endearing—characteristic: at any call or
whistle he would look in precisely the opposite
direction How many times all through his
life have I not seen him, at my whistle, start
violently and turn his tail to me, then, with
nose thrown searchingly from side to side,
begin to canter toward the horizon!

In that first walk, we met, fortunately, but
one vehicle, a brewer's dray; he chose that
moment to attend to the more serious affairs of
life, sitting quietly before the horses' feet and
requiring to be moved by hand. From the
beginning he had his dignity, and was extremely
difficult to lift, owing to the length of his
middle distance.

What strange feelings must have stirred in
his little white soul when he first smelled

"At a call or whistle he would look in precisely

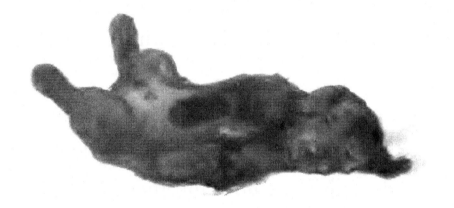

Maud Earl

" Keeping me too warm down my back."

carpet! But it was all so strange to him that day—I doubt if he felt more than I did when I first travelled to my private school, reading "Tales of a Grandfather," and plied with tracts and sherry by my father's man of business

That night, indeed, for several nights, he slept with me, keeping me too warm down my back, and waking me now and then with quaint sleepy whimperings Indeed, all through his life he flew a good deal in his sleep, fighting dogs and seeing ghosts, running after rabbits and thrown sticks; and to the last one never quite knew whether or no to rouse him when his four black feet began to jerk and quiver. His dreams were like our dreams, both good and bad; happy sometimes, sometimes tragic to weeping point.

MEMORIES

He ceased to sleep with me the day we discovered that he was a perfect little colony, whose settlers were of an active species which I have never seen again. After that he had many beds, for circumstance ordained that his life should be nomadic, and it is to this I trace that philosophic indifference to place or property, which marked him out from most of his own kind. He learned early that for a black dog with long silky ears, a feathered tail, and head of great dignity, there was no home whatsoever, away from those creatures with special scents, who took liberties with his name, and alone of all created things were privileged to smack him with a slipper. He would sleep anywhere, so long as it was in their room, or so close outside it as to make no matter, for it was with him a principle that what he did not

Maud Earl.

" And alone of all created things were privileged to
smack him with a slipper."

smell did not exist. I would I could hear again those long rubber-lipped snufflings of recognition underneath the door, with which each morning he would regale and reassure a spirit that grew with age more and more nervous and delicate about this matter of propinquity! For he was a dog of fixed ideas, things stamped on his mind were indelible; as, for example, his duty toward cats, for whom he had really a perverse affection, which had led to that first disastrous moment of his life, when he was brought up, poor bewildered puppy, from a brief excursion to the kitchen, with one eye closed and his cheek torn! He bore to his grave that jagged scratch across the eye. It was in dread of a repetition of this tragedy that he was instructed at the word "Cats" to rush forward with a special "tow-row-rowing," which he

'Should I could hear again those long

never used toward any other form of creature. To the end he cherished a hope that he would reach the cat, but never did; and if he had, we knew he would only have stood and wagged his tail; but I well remember once, when he returned, important, from some such sally, how dreadfully my companion startled a cat-loving friend by murmuring in her most honeyed voice: "Well, my darling, have you been killing pussies in the garden?"

His eye and nose were impeccable in their sense of form; indeed, he was very English in that matter· people must be just so; things smell properly; and affairs go on in the one right way He could tolerate neither creatures in ragged clothes, nor children on their hands and knees, nor postmen, because, with their bags, they swelled-up on one side,

Maud Earl

"He would never let the harmless creatures pass without religious barks."

and carried lanterns on their stomachs. He would never let the harmless creatures pass without religious barks. Naturally a believer in authority and routine, and distrusting spiritual adventure, he yet had curious fads that seemed to have nested in him, quite outside of all principle. He would, for instance, follow neither carriages nor horses, and if we tried to make him, at once left for home, where he would sit with nose raised to heaven, emitting through it a most lugubrious, shrill noise. Then again, one must not place a stick, a slipper, a glove, or anything with which he could play, upon one's head—since such an action reduced him at once to frenzy. For so conservative a dog, his environment was sadly anarchistic. He never complained in words of our shifting habits, but curled his head round over his left

Maud Earl

"Emitting through it a most lugubrious, shrill noise."

paw and pressed his chin very hard against the ground whenever he smelled packing What necessity,—he seemed continually to be saying, —what real necessity is there for change of any kind whatever? Here we were all together, and one day was like another, so that I knew where I was—and now *you* only know what will happen next; and *I*—I can't tell you whether I shall be with you when it happens! What strange, grieving minutes a dog passes at such times in the underground of his subconsciousness, refusing realization, yet all the time only too well divining. Some careless word, some unmuted compassion in voice, the stealthy wrapping of a pair of boots, the unaccustomed shutting of a door that ought to be open, the removal from a down-stair room of an object always there—one tiny thing, and he

"Chin very hard against the ground whenever he smelled
[...]"

knows for certain that he is not going too. He fights against the knowledge just as we do against what we cannot bear; he gives up hope, but not effort, protesting in the only way he knows of, and now and then heaving a great sigh. Those sighs of a dog! They go to the heart so much more deeply than the sighs of our own kind, because they are utterly unintended, regardless of effect, emerging from one who, heaving them, knows not that they have escaped him!

The words: "Yes—going too!" spoken in a certain tone, would call up in his eyes a still-questioning half-happiness, and from his tail a quiet flutter, but did not quite serve to put to rest either his doubt or his feeling that it was all unnecessary—until the cab arrived. Then he would pour himself out of door or

"Would be found in the bottom of the vehicle".

MEMORIES

window, and be found in the bottom of the vehicle, looking severely away from an admiring cabman. Once settled on our feet he travelled with philosophy, but no digestion.

I think no dog was ever more indifferent to an outside world of human creatures; yet few dogs have made more conquests—especially among strange women, through whom, however, he had a habit of looking—very discouraging. He had, natheless, one or two particular friends, such as him to whom this book is dedicated, and a few persons whom he knew he had seen before, but, broadly speaking, there were in his world of men, only his mistress and—the almighty.

Each August, till he was six, he was sent for health, and the assuagement of his hereditary instincts, up to a Scotch shooting, where he

carried many birds in a very tender manner.
Once he was compelled by Fate to remain
there nearly a year; and we went up ourselves
to fetch him home. Down the long avenue
toward the keeper's cottage we walked. It
was high autumn; there had been frost already,
for the ground was fine with red and yellow
leaves, and presently we saw himself coming,
professionally questing among those leaves, and
preceding his dear keeper with the business-
like self-containment of a sportsman; not too
fat, glossy as a raven's wing, swinging his ears
and sporran like a little Highlander. We
approached him silently. Suddenly his nose
went up from its imagined trail, and he came
rushing at our legs. From him, as a garment
drops from a man, dropped all his strange
soberness; he became in a single instant

" Where he carried many birds and hares

one fluttering eagerness. He leaped from life to life in one bound, without hesitation, without regret. Not one sigh, not one look back, not the faintest token of gratitude or regret at leaving those good people who had tended him for a whole year, buttered oat-cake for him, allowed him to choose each night exactly where he would sleep. No, he just marched out beside us, as close as ever he could get, drawing us on in spirit, and not even attending to the scents, until the lodge gates were passed.

It was strictly in accordance with the perversity of things, and something in the nature of calamity that he had not been ours one year, when there came over me a dreadful but overmastering aversion from killing those birds and creatures of which he was so fond as soon as they were dead. And so I never knew him as

MEMORIES

a sportsman: for during that first year he was only an unbroken puppy, tied to my waist for fear of accidents, and carefully pulling me off every shot. They tell me he developed a lovely nose and perfect mouth, large enough to hold gingerly the biggest hare. I well believe it, remembering the qualities of his mother, whose character, however, in stability he far surpassed. But, as *he* grew every year more devoted to dead grouse and birds and rabbits, *I* liked them more and more alive; it was the only real breach between us, and we kept it out of sight. Ah! well; it is consoling to reflect that I should infallibly have ruined his sporting qualities, lacking that peculiar habit of meaning what one says, so necessary to keep dogs virtuous. But surely to have had him with me, quivering and alert, with his

" Carefully putting me off every shot."

solemn, eager face, would have given a new joy
to those crisp mornings when the hope of
wings coming to the gun makes poignant in
the sportsman as nothing else will, an almost
sensual love of Nature, a fierce delight in the
soft glow of leaves, in the white birch stems and
tracery of sparse twigs against blue sky, in the
scents of sap and grass and gum and heather
flowers; stivers the hair of him with keenness
for interpreting each sound, and fills the very
fern or moss he kneels on, the very trunk
he leans against, with strange vibration

Slowly Fate prepares for each of us the
religion that lies coiled in our most secret
nerves; with such we cannot trifle, we do not
even try!   But how shall a man grudge any
one sensations he has so keenly felt?   Let such
as have never known those curious delights,

uphold the hand of horror—for me there can be no such luxury. If I could, I would still perhaps be knowing them; but when once the joy of life in those winged and furry things has knocked at the very portals of one's spirit, the thought that by pressing a little iron twig one will rive that joy out of their vitals, is too hard to bear. Call it æstheticism, squeamishness, namby-pamby sentimentalism, what you will— it is stronger than oneself!

Yes, after one had once watched with an eye that did not merely see, the thirsty gaping of a slowly dying bird, or a rabbit dragging a broken leg to a hole where he would lie for hours thinking of the fern to which he should never more come forth—after that, there was always the following little matter of arithmetic: Given, that all those who had been shooting were "good-fair" shots—which, Heaven knew, they never were—they yet missed one at least in four, and did not miss it very much; so that if seventy-five things were slain, there were also twenty-five that had been fired at, and, of those twenty-five, twelve and a half had "gotten it" somewhere in their bodies, and would "likely" die at their great leisure.

This was the sum that brought about the only cleavage in our lives; and so, as he grew older, and trying to part from each other we no longer could, he ceased going to Scotland. But after that I often felt, and especially when we heard guns, how the best and most secret instincts of him were being stifled. But what was to be done? In that which was left of a clay pigeon he would take not the faintest interest—the scent of it was paltry. Yet always, even in his most cosseted and idle days, he managed to preserve the grave preoccupation of one professionally concerned with retrieving things that smell; and consoled himself with pastimes such as cricket, which he played in a manner highly specialized, following the ball up the moment it left the bowler's hand, and sometimes retrieving it before it reached the batsman. When remonstrated with, he would consider a little, hanging out a pink tongue and looking rather too eagerly at the ball, then canter slowly out to a sort of forward short leg. Why he always chose that particular position is difficult to say; possibly he could lurk there better than anywhere else, the batsman's eye not being on him, and the bowler's not too much. As a fieldsman he was perfect, but for an occasional belief that he was

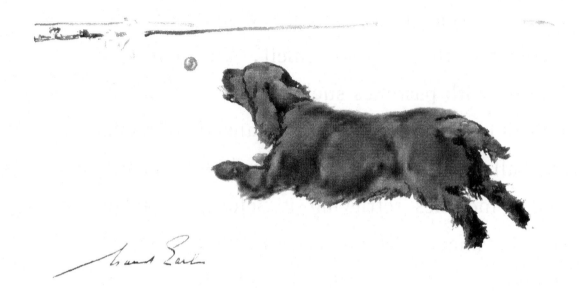

"Following the ball up the moment it left the bowler's hand,"

"When remonstrated with, he would consider a little,"

not merely short leg, but slip, point, mid-off, and wicket-keep; and perhaps a tendency to make the ball a little "jubey." But he worked tremendously, watching every movement, for he knew the game thoroughly, and seldom delayed it more than three minutes when he secured the ball And if that ball were really lost, then indeed he took over the proceedings with an intensity and quiet vigour that destroyed many shrubs, and the solemn satisfaction which comes from being in the very centre of the stage.

But his most passionate delight was swimming in anything except the sea, for which, with its unpleasant noise and habit of tasting salt, he had little affection. I see him now, cleaving the Serpentine, with his air of "the world well lost," striving to reach my stick before it had touched water. Being only a large spaniel, too

small for mere heroism, he saved no lives in the
water but his own—and that, on one occasion,
before our very eyes, from a dark trout stream,
which was trying to wash him down into a
black hole among the boulders

The call of the wild—Spring running—
whatever it is—that besets men and dogs,
seldom attained full mastery over him; but one
could often see it struggling against his devotion
to the scent of us, and, watching that dumb
contest, I have time and again wondered how
far this civilization of ours was justifiably im-
posed on him; how far the love for us that
we had so carefully implanted could ever replace
in him the satisfaction of his primitive wild
yearnings. He was like a man, naturally
polygamous, married to one loved woman.

It was surely not for nothing that Rover is

" But his most passionate delight was Swimming.

dog's most common name, and would be ours, but for our too tenacious fear of losing something, to admit, even to ourselves, that we are hankering. There was a man who said: Strange that two such queerly opposite qualities as courage and hypocrisy are the leading characteristics of the Anglo-Saxon! But is not hypocrisy just a product of tenacity, which is again the lower part of courage? Is not hypocrisy but an active sense of property in one's good name, the clutching close of respectability at any price, the feeling that one must not part, even at the cost of truth, with what he has sweated so to gain? And so we Anglo-Saxons will not answer to the name of Rover, and treat our dogs so that they, too, hardly know their natures.

The history of his one wandering, for which

no respectable reason can be assigned, will never, of course, be known. It was in London, of an October evening, when we were told he had slipped out and was not anywhere. Then began those four distressful hours of searching for that black needle in that blacker bundle of hay. Hours of real dismay and suffering—for it is suffering, indeed, to feel a loved thing swallowed up in that hopeless maze of London streets Stolen or run over? Which was worse? The neighbouring police stations visited, the Dog's Home notified, an order for five hundred "Lost Dog" bills placed in the printer's hands, the streets patrolled! And then, in a lull snatched for food, and still endeavouring to preserve some aspect of assurance, we heard the bark which meant: " Here is a door I cannot open!" We hurried forth, and there

" ... ... on the toh doorstep — busy, unashamed,"

asleep, for he knew not remorse."

he was on the top doorstep—busy, unashamed, giving no explanations, asking for his supper; and very shortly after him came his five hundred " Lost Dog " bills   Long I sat looking at him that night after my companion had gone up, thinking of the evening, some years before, when there followed us that shadow of a spaniel who had been lost for eleven days.   And my heart turned over within me.   But he!   He was asleep, for he knew not remorse.

Ah! and there was that other time, when it was reported to me, returning home at night, that he had gone out to find me; and I went forth again, disturbed, and whistling his special call to the empty fields.   Suddenly out of the darkness I heard a rushing, and he came furiously dashing against my heels from he alone knew where he had been lurking and saying to

" Rushing piece of blackness, through the blacker night."

himself: I will not go in till he comes! I could not scold, there was something too lyrical in the return of that live, lonely, rushing piece of blackness through the blacker night After all, the vagary was but a variation in his practice when one was away at bed-time, of passionately scratching up his bed in protest, till it resembled nothing; for, in spite of his long and solemn face and the silkiness of his ears, there was much in him yet of the cave bear—he dug graves on the smallest provocations, in which he never buried anything. He was not a " clever " dog; and guiltless of all tricks. Nor was he ever " shown " We did not even dream of subject-ing him to this indignity. Was our dog a clown, a hobby, a fad, a fashion, a feather in our caps—that we should subject him to periodic pennings in stuffy halls, that we should harry his faithful soul with such tomfoolery? He never even heard us talk about his lineage, deplore the length of his nose, or call him "clever-looking." We should have been ashamed to let him smell about us the tar-brush of a sense of property, to let him think we looked on him as an asset to earn us pelf or glory. We wished that there should be between us the spirit that was between the sheep-dog and that farmer, who, when asked his dog's age, touched the old creature's head, and answered thus: "Teresa" (his daughter) "was born in November, and this one in August." That sheep-dog had seen eighteen years when the great white day came for him, and his spirit passed away up, to cling with the wood-smoke round the dark rafters of the kitchen where he had lain so vast a time beside his master's boots.

"He dug graves on the smallest provocation."

MEMORIES

No, no! If a man does not soon pass beyond the thought: " By what shall this dog profit me?" into the large state of simple gladness to be with dog, he shall never know the very essence of that companionship which depends not on the points of dog, but on some strange and subtle mingling of mute spirits For it is by muteness that a dog becomes for one so utterly beyond value; with him one is at peace, where words play no torturing tricks. When he just sits, loving, and knows that he is being loved, those are the moments that I think are precious to a dog, when, with his adoring soul coming through his eyes, he feels that you are really thinking of him But he is touchingly tolerant of one's other occupations. The subject of these memories always knew when one was too absorbed in work to be so close to

" When he just sits loving

him as he thought proper; yet he never tried
to hinder or distract, or asked for attention. It
dinged his mood, of course, so that the red
under his eyes and the folds of his crumply
cheeks—which seemed to speak of a touch of
bloodhound introduced a long way back into
his breeding—grew deeper and more manifest.
If he could have spoken at such times, he
would have said: "I have been a long time
alone, and I cannot always be asleep; but you
know best, and I must not criticise."

He did not at all mind one's being absorbed
in other humans; he seemed to enjoy the
sounds of conversation lifting round him, and
to know when they were sensible. He could
not, for instance, stand actors or actresses
giving readings of their parts, perceiving at
once that the same had no connection with the

minds and real feelings of the speakers; and, having wandered a little to show his disapproval, he would go to the door and stare at it till it opened and let him out Once or twice, it is true, when an actor of large voice was declaiming an emotional passage, he so far relented as to go up to him and pant in his face. Music, too, made him restless, inclined to sigh, and to ask questions Sometimes, at its first sound, he would cross to the window and remain there looking for Her. At others, he would simply go and lie on the loud pedal, and we never could tell whether it was from sentiment, or because he thought that in this way he heard less. At one special Nocturne of Chopin's he always whimpered He *was*, indeed, of rather Polish temperament—very gay when he was gay, dark and brooding when he was not.

MEMORIES

On the whole, perhaps his life was uneventful for so far-travelling a dog, though it held its moments of eccentricity, as when he leaped through the window of a four-wheeler into Kensington, or sat on a Dartmoor adder. But that was fortunately of a Sunday afternoon —when adder and all were torpid, so nothing happened, till a friend, who was following, lifted him off the creature with his large boot.

If only one could have known more of his private life—more of his relations with his own kind! I fancy he was always rather a dark dog to them, having so many thoughts about us that he could not share with any one, and being naturally fastidious, except with ladies, for whom he had a chivalrous and catholic taste, so that they often turned and snapped at him. He had, however, but one lasting love affair,

for a liver-coloured lass of our village, not quite of his own caste, but a wholesome if somewhat elderly girl, with loving and sphinx-like eyes. Their children, alas, were not for this world, and soon departed.

Nor was he a fighting dog; but once attacked, he lacked a sense of values, being unable to distinguish between dogs that he could beat and dogs with whom he had " no earthly." It was, in fact, as well to interfere at once, especially in the matter of retrievers, for he never forgot having in his youth been attacked by a retriever from behind No, he never forgot, and never forgave, an enemy. Only a month before that day of which I cannot speak, being very old and ill, he engaged an Irish terrier on whose impudence he had long had his eye, and routed him. And how a battle

"Being very old and ill, he engaged an Irish terrier

cheered his spirit! He was certainly no Christian; but, allowing for essential dog, he was very much a gentleman. And I do think that most of us who live on this earth these days would rather leave it with that label on us than the other. For to be a Christian, as Tolstoy understood the word—and no one else in our time has had logic and love of truth enough to give it coherent meaning—is (to be quite sincere) not suited to men of Western blood. Whereas—to be a gentleman! It is a far cry, but perhaps it can be done. In him, at all events, there was no pettiness, no meanness, and no cruelty, and though he fell below his ideal at times, this never altered the true look of his eyes, nor the simple loyalty in his soul.

But what a crowd of memories come back, bringing with them the perfume of fallen days!

MEMORIES

What delights and glamour, what long hours of effort, discouragements, and secret fears did he not watch over—our black familiar; and with the sight and scent and touch of him, deepen or assuage! How many thousand walks did we not go together, so that we still turn to see if he is following at his padding gait, attentive to the invisible trails. Not the least hard thing to bear when they go from us, these quiet friends, is that they carry away with them so many years of our own lives. Yet, if they find warmth therein, who would grudge them those years that they have so guarded? Nothing else of us can they take to lie upon with outstretched paws and chin pressed to the ground; and, whatever they take, be sure they have deserved.

Do they know, as we do, that their time must come? Yes, they know, at rare moments

"So that was still turn to see if he is following at his padding gait."

MEMORIES

No other way can I interpret those pauses of his latter life, when, propped on his forefeet, he would sit for long minutes quite motionless —his head drooped, utterly withdrawn, then turn those eyes of his and look at me. That look said more plainly than all words could: "Yes, I know that I must go!" If *we* have spirits that persist—*they* have. If *we* know after our departure, who we were—*they* do. No one, I think, who really longs for truth, can ever glibly say which it will be for dog and man—persistence or extinction of our consciousness. There is but one thing certain— the childishness of fretting over that eternal question. Whichever it be, it must be right, the only possible thing. He felt that too, I know; but then, like his master, he was what is called a pessimist.

MEMORIES

My companion tells me that, since he left us, he has once come back. It was Old Year's Night, and she was sad, when he came to her in visible shape of his black body, passing round the dining-table from the window-end, to his proper place beneath the table, at her feet. She saw him quite clearly; she heard the padding tap-tap of his paws and very toe-nails; she felt his warmth brushing hard against the front of her skirt. She thought then that he would settle down upon her feet, but something disturbed him, and he stood pausing, pressed against her, then moved out toward where I generally sit, but was not sitting that night She saw him stand there, as if considering; then at some sound or laugh, she became self-conscious, and slowly, very slowly, he was no longer there. Had he some message, some

MEMORIES

counsel to give, something he would say, that last night of the last year of all those he had watched over us?   Will he come back again?

No stone stands over where he lies.   It is on our hearts that his life is engraved.

1912

Lightning Source UK Ltd.
Milton Keynes UK
UKOW07f0645220517

301726UK00010B/650/P